There Is Still Time

A poet's journey to becoming Peace and Calm
The real, raw, broken, brave path of life

Heartfully Written

By Lauren Emily Whitesell

This book was written in honor of my dad on his 60th
birthday—

the person who first inspired my love of poetry,
language, and the quiet magic hidden inside words.

But perhaps it was always meant for more than one
person.

For anyone who has ever questioned how they arrived
where they are.

For anyone wondering if there is still time—

to change,
to become,
to make a difference,
to live in accordance with the dreams quietly living
inside of them.

I hope these pages remind you:

there is still time

Who We Want to Be

Each Morning,
The birds sing their songs.

Each Evening,
They return home.

Each different,
Each special in their own way.

What music their singing
Brings our souls.

What healing can they offer us?

How do the sound of their voices
Rise up?
Rise through the airwaves?

How can we hear their messages?

How can we know they
Carry Love?

What does each song mean?
What does each flight bring?

How can it unlock my heart?
How can it bring me back to my soul?

The notes of each song,
Each bird,
Each flight

Different in their own way
Yet they are in the same sky.

Bringing about Light

Dawn,
Spring,
Renewal,
Peace.

What joy their warmth
Brings

What love their voices
Sing

What hope their messages
Soar within.

Up into the cosmos
Up into our hearts

Unearthing the hidden pieces of
Who we are
Who we want to be

The birds have their own song,
We all have our own songs
Together we honor our unique songs

Because together we can make
Beautiful
Music.

The Art of Stillness

What is stillness?

It's a quieting
Of the Outside World

So you can sit
With your soul.

To hear the wisdom within,
To heal.

The practice of stillness,
Is to be gentle with yourself.

Allow softness in,
Allow quiet stillness,

Allow the sounds of the world around you
To infiltrate your senses

Be the beacon of Light
That you are

Be guided by the heart,
YOUR heart

Yo Yo of the Heart

Everything is connected
Yet it feels so disconnected

How can it toy
Between the two–

Like a yo yo of the heart

Time Is a Bandit

Time is a bandit

Stealing from you
Moments of
Joy and Heartache

Wanting you
To yearn for
Brighter days,
Easier days,

Yet keeping you
Present
In the moment

Soaking up
All the
Rays of
Sunshine,
Of Light

Until you are
Bursting at
The seams

Light pouring
Over
And out

Igniting the way
To your soul,
To your heart.

The Pursuit of More

Time has a funny way
Of running away from us

Yet slinking by like a snail

Slow and steady,
Fast and in a blur

It's a bandit

Stealing from us what we crave the most:

Moments,
Memories

In one moment and
Out the next

It's the quiet times

We spend
Contemplating,
Reflecting,
Reminiscing

That reminds us
To soak it up–
To live in the moments
That define us

Not to live the life that is gone,
Never to return

These are what make a life:

These memories
These moments

Of gentleness,
Of sorrow,
Of pain,
Of heartache,
Of LOVE

These are the things we live for
In our pursuit for more

More freedom,
More love,
More money,
More,
More,
More

But it's really more
TIME
We are after

More moments to make a difference
More memories of LIFE

Child of God

Time and space
The gentleness of peace

Of quiet solitude,
Of remembering

It beacons us,
Calls to our soul.

Be patient,
Be quiet, sweet child.

My light is within you,
My light is all around you.

Listen to its whispers,
Can you hear it?

Find the peace and calm
In the chaos of everyday life,
Of everyday monotony.

Question your existence

Quiet the doubt,
Listen to your soul.

It has the messages you are seeking

Do not diminish them.
Do not soften your light.

Do not let the world
Allow you to forget who you are,
What you are

You are a Child of God

What if God Wasn't a Man?

What if God wasn't a man?

But was as fluid
As the air we breathe

As ever changing
As the water
That courses through us

What if God was all around us?

In quiet moments,
In soft embraces,
In warmth and love

What if God was within us?

Loving us,
Begging us to see
What is inside of us

What if God wasn't
A man
Or a woman

What if we are GOD?

Seasons of Growth

Seasons.
The ebb and flow,
Like the never ending
Pulse of Life.

Cycles come and go,
Adapt and renew.

Release.
Breathe.
Inhale.
Exhale.

Smooth and soft.
Gentle and calm.

Open yourself to
The Possibilities,
The Potential,
The Achievable,
The Growth.

Mindless scrolling,
Lost control in
My Self.

Getting back to the core
Of it all.

Gentleness
With ourselves,
With others,

With our bodies.

Heal and grow,
Learn and adapt

We make choices
That affect our mind,
Our body,
Our soul

Discretion,
Softness

Allow the ebb and flow
To pull at you like
A schoolyard swing

Billowing in the wind's kiss
Never forgotten,
Just lost the map back.

Elixir of the Soul

Drinking up

The solitude,
The quiet,
The peace

To ensure my
Body,
Mind,
Soul

Can take on the
Chaos
Again

Renewed,
Rejuvenated

And ready for LOVE
Ready for LIGHT.
Ready to GUIDE
And TEACH
And open for
MORE

More Knowledge,
More Light,
More Love,
More Freedom,
More Adventure,
More Laughter,
More Comfort from the Darkness.

Let Our Children Ignite Us

Let our children
Ignite us,
Lift us up

Rather than weigh us
Down.

The balance of

Light and Darkness,
Laughter and Love,
Freedom and Responsibility.

Let our children
Connect us,
Fuel us.

To be the best version of
Ourselves

To teach them to
Be better versions of
Themselves.

So they can Light up
This World

With their big
Strong
LIGHT

Caverns of My Heart

The caverns of my heart
Broken

Holding the weight of the world

The cruelty,
And uncertainty,
The pain and sadness

Deep Oceans

The vastness of your oceans
Sucking me into their vortex

All knowing

Bluer than the cloudless sky
Brighter than the beaming sun

Your suit of armor
As soft as a pussywillow
As fragile as a bowl made of glass

The sweetness of your voice
Like birds arriving to announce spring's return
Singing the song of my heart

The gentleness of your soul
Easing every tension in my body
Releasing all worries and expectations

Easing into the flow
Of the River of Life

The Way to Trust Our Hearts

Quiet solitude,
Peaceful heart
A great pause.

Sometimes we feel
We must
Talk to talk

But what if we stopped to pause?

And truly listen to the sounds of our Soul
Calling to us?

Would we hear it calling to
The Wind?

Allow the gentle Breeze
To wash over
Our troubles

To soften our desire
For more,
For control.

What if we surrender
To the Unknown
Mysteries of life?

What if we trust
In the Divine plan?

What if we lead

With Love?
With Life?

The Wise Mother
Calls us to sit in
Her Light–

A Great Peace.

The gentleness of her touch,
The soft embrace of
Her Love.

Let it rise up from within

We must dive deeply
Into the Soul to find
Her Power,

To shine Her Love for the world
To SEE

Let us break open our Minds,
Our Hearts,
To see what we cannot fathom
To understand,
Only that which we must trust.

Trust our hearts–
They will lead The Way

The Shape Left Behind

I can feel myself transforming

A cracking open
Of my soul

A birth,
A return to self.

Can you feel it too?

A bud on the tree
Of life

An emergence
Of the long awaited
Spring.

The clouds parting way
For your light to
Shine

Bright as the sun,
Beaming,
Glowing

For all to see
To uncover
Their light

To shine
Through the darkness
Of tragedy
And sorrow

The hollow ache
Of your heart

Urging you
Back inside
To your soul,
Your true essence.

The shape left behind,
Your shadow

Dusting off
The cobwebs of
Your heart
To illuminate
The path forward,
The path home

Let the Wind

The trees rise up
Rooted In the green

Wings flutter by
A gentle whisper
In the leaves

Cleansing,
Renewing,
Healing

Ground into Mother Gaia,
Release all your pain to Her

Green rising up,
Rooting up through
The ten little toes
That tie you to
Your feet

Let them bring you forward,
Towards growth,
Towards healing

Let the breeze wash away
The heartbreak,
The pain,
The sorrow

Of years passed,
Of lives lived

Let the sounds
Of Nature,
Of Earth
Calm you the way
A mothers breast calms
A crying infant

Ask Her to sing you
Songs of your soul

Ask Her to carry away
All that is on your heart

Ask Her to bring back
The joy,
The laughter,
The love

Be gentle with your Soul,
Your Self

Do not question when it falters
But sit with it

Like an old familiar friend,
Like the Grandmother Willow
Billowing in the wind

Release to Her
What you cannot
See for yourself

What pains you,
What makes your heart soar

Let the wind wash over you
Let your toes wiggle in the grass
Let the songs of nature,
Of the birds
Sing to your Soul

Roots of Creation

The wildflowers bend
With the gentle sway,
The tears of the sky
Weighing them down
Forcing them back into
The dirt.

Yet they rise–

Stronger,
Healthier,

More rooted in
The softness of the soil

Like our spirits
In our bodies,

Tethered to the
Roots of Creation
Yet grounded in density.

Feeling heavy,
And weighed down
By the world,
Yet strong
And resilient.

I Am A Poet

I am a poet.

My heart sings the words,
It soars through the ethers,
To the pages I write

I am a poet.

Floating through time and space,
Space and time,
To bring wisdom
To the world

I am a poet.

The words I write,
The feelings inside,
Bursting from the page,
Enveloping us in love

I am a poet.

Rise Up from the Ashes

Be gentle with your Soul
As it transforms

Let it wash over you
With its gentle breath

Finding ourselves
In the lost chaos
Of everyday life

Struggling to keep
Our heads above water,
Our hearts on shore.

The wave of who I used to BE
Washes over me,

Reflecting back what
No longer serves me.

Transmuted and transformed,
Sprinkling its joy softly on my lips

Quiet introspection
Resets the path forward–

The path home to Self,
Transforming,
Growing.

Always evolving,
Awakening.

The lost fragments of myself
Shining,

Guiding me along,
Leading the way
Home.

Renewed,
Rejuvenated
And Refreshed

Grieving the shape I once inhabited,
Knowing I cannot return–

Yet She's stronger now,
More resilient,

Eager to change and grow,
Expand and explore
All that life brings with it.

A remembering,
A revival of who
I AM.

Let her rise up from the ashes
Of the storm.

Let her feel her power, her strength–
Let her root into her Soul, at last.

The Crawl

Life is like crawling,
Always striving for more
Yet being content
With where we are

It's about patience,
And perseverance.

It's about getting back up
When we fall.

We stretch out our arms
And reach further,
Higher–

Until either we fall
Flat on our face
Or succeed.

But we keep trying,
Over and over
Again.

Making progress,
Then falling back.

Getting up on all fours,
And falling back–

Until one day
We get up and walk.

Confident and strong,
Resilient and bold,

Tactful yet poignant.

Life is chaos an overwhelm,
Beauty and peace.

It's not perfection,
But striving for more–

More joy,
More love,
More happiness.

More peace,
More calm.

More beauty,
More magic.

Life is beautiful
And powerful
And difficult
And overwhelming–

But it is so damn MAGICAL.

Can you see it too?

Pain is An Illusion

All pain is an illusion
But pain is not the illusion.

The notion that we ARE the pain
Is the illusion we must face.

In order to move through it,
We must FEEL the pain.

We must allow it to
Flow like the waves of the ocean,
Rather than the depths of the sea
Threatening to swallow us whole.

By feeling the pain,
We can begin to understand it,
Recognize it,
Identify it.

And know that we are NOT the pain.
We will NOT become it.

As long as we let it move through us,
Teaching us
How to let go.

Be Gentle With Your Soul

Be gentle with your Soul
As it navigates this season,

The constant
Ebb and flow
Of Life

Be gentle with your Soul

As it heals and learns,
It takes time for these things.

Be gentle with your Soul.

You do not need to be on
Any timeline but your own.

Be gentle with your Soul,
Be easy with your Self,
And go with the flow.

Forget the shoulds,
The coulds,
The would-haves.

And just BE.

Tides change each day,
And so can you.

Be gentle with your Soul,
It takes time to grow.

Let yourself feel.
Let yourself cry.
Let yourself be.

Be rooted in the soil,
Water your Spirit.

Let the Sun shine Light
Into your Being.

Let the Moon reveal
Your Shadow

Be gentle with your Soul.

The Art of Being in Flow

In life we are always pursuing,
Always wanting more

But to be in flow,
We must be one with the cycles
Of nature,
Of the world around us

Slow and steady,
Things take time to grow

They need nurturing
They need love

How are you showing yourself
Love today?

Heart Whispers

There comes a day when
The body turns to dust,
Yet the Spirit remains

Enveloping us in LOVE,
Like a blanket of comfort.

Gentle and smooth,
With the old familiar scent
Of their energy,
Their essence,
Ever present

Often we feel
Lost when they cannot be
SEEN

But that's where the true magic
LIVES

In moments of heartache
And despair,
Our heart shows us
The truth
To the mystery of life

We cannot see,
We cannot hear,
We cannot fear,

What is just beyond our reach
But we TRUST

It is there

We KNOW
It is hiding in the shadows

Only our hearts
Can reveal

Listen closely to the heart whispers,
The wisdom She holds
Brings
MAGIC

Love Connects Us All

We often think about what life
Will be like
In one year,
Five years,
Ten years,
Twenty years

We get caught up in
The next thing,
The next stage,

But what if we take a MOMENT
And truly BE in the NOW?

How could that transform us?

The moments we let ourselves
Think about the future
Can both excite us
And sadden us

We inadvertently wish away
What could be the most magical moments

We see past the struggles,
The heartache of life
And wish to speed things up

To have the next season
Envelop us

But isn't this part of the human journey?

Exploring the ebbs and flows of life,
Enjoying the changing seasons,
The growth and change
We endure as human beings

Living in the NOW is
Honoring the journey,
The changes,
The loss,
The love
And everything in between

It's wishing away moments
Then regretting them,
Instantly remorseful,

It's sending grace and love
To all parts of us.

Not just the good
But the bad and ugly too

It's protecting and loving
Our SOVEREIGNTY

It's finding our SOUL
Along the journey

Remembering to
Inhale courage in the darker moments
And exhale fear in the lighter moments

Breath gives us life

Moments keep us moving forward

Love connects us all

There Is Still Time

To the one who showed me the love of writing poetry +
the joy in sharing with others
On your 60th birthday, August 20, 2022

Sixty and seven months.
What a joy it is to watch
Your children become parents,
Your parents become grandparents.

Watching the joy
In the eyes of the beholder
Knowing the bonds and love
They build together,
Trusting in all that is
And ever will be

As we get older,
Closer to the end,
We reflect on the life
We lived.

Was it joyous?
Was there misery?
Was there hope
And love?

Did we fulfill our passions?

There is still time.

Time to soak in the moments,
Time to make new memories,
Time to live life the way

We want to
Rather than the way we feel
We should.

As we age, we feel more
Disappointed
In all that was potentially
Squandered.

But what if all these
Roadblocks,
Heartaches,
And troubles
Were to get us here,
In this moment

The moment we realized

There is still so much TIME.

Time to pursue our dreams,
To live in the moment,
To find passion,
And joy,
And love

There is still so much time.

To be who we are meant to be,
To follow our hearts desires,
To listen to the calling within

There is still so much time.

To find joy in the mundane,
To seek love where it has faltered.

There is still so much time.

On this day, my hope for you
Is that you remember your
Innate beauty

What makes you human?

What brings you joy?

What awakens your soul?

Can you hear his whispers?
What is he calling you to do?

Be present,
Listen closely

Patience.
Silence.
Trust.
Surrender.

All Will Be Well.

About the Author

Lauren Whitesell is a poet, mother, and lifelong observer of the quiet beauty and complexity of being human.

Her writing explores healing, becoming, grief, hope, love, and the tender spaces in between—capturing the lived experience of growth, self-trust, and returning to ourselves through life's many seasons.

She lives in New Hampshire with her daughters, where much of her inspiration is found in nature, memory, and the everyday magic hidden inside ordinary moments.